Fermentation for Beginners

Easy and Tasty Recipes for Sauerkraut, Pickles, Kimchi, Salsa, and More

Melanie Bennet

© **Text Copyright 2022 by Melanie Bennet - All rights reserved.**

This document is geared towards providing exact and reliable information in regards to the topic and issue covered. The publication is sold with the idea that the publisher or author is not required to render accounting, officially permitted, or otherwise, qualified services. If advice is necessary, legal or professional, a practiced individual in the profession should be ordered.

From a Declaration of Principles which was accepted and approved equally by a Committee of the American Bar Association and a Committee of Publishers and Associations.

In no way is it legal to reproduce, duplicate, or transmit any part of this document in either electronic means or in printed format. Recording of this publication is strictly prohibited and any storage of this document is not allowed unless with written permission from the publisher. All rights reserved.

The information provided herein is stated to be truthful and consistent, in that any liability, in terms of inattention or otherwise, by any usage or abuse of any policies, processes, or directions contained within is the solitary and utter responsibility of the recipient reader. By reading this document, the reader agrees that under no circumstances will any legal responsibility or blame be held against the publisher, or author, for any reparation, damages, or monetary loss due to the information herein, either directly or indirectly.

Respective authors own all copyrights not held by the publisher.

The information herein is offered for informational purposes solely, and is universal as so. The presentation of the information is without contract or any type of guarantee assurance.

The trademarks that are used are without any consent, and the publication of the trademark is without permission or backing by the trademark owner. All trademarks and brands within this book are for clarifying purposes only and are owned by the owners themselves, not affiliated with this document.

Table of Contents

Introduction 1

CHAPTER ONE

Why Ferment Vegetables: Understanding Health Benefits 3

    A History Lesson 3
    The Reasoning Behind Fermentation 4
    Health Benefits 5

CHAPTER TWO

How to Ferment Vegetables at Home 7

    The Factors 7
        Water 7
        Salt 8
        Cultures 9
    Creating the Conditions 9
    Equipment 10
        Containers 10
        Weights and a Thermometer 11
    Preparing and Storing the Food 12
    Precautions and Troubleshooting 13

CHAPTER THREE

How to Make Sauerkraut 15

    Basic Sauerkraut Recipe 15
    Variation Recipes 17
        Carrot Kraut 17
        Salt-free Kraut 17

CHAPTER FOUR

How to Make Pickles and Relishes 19
    Cucumber Pickles 19
    Pickled Watermelon Rind 21
    Pickled Onions 22
    Relishes 22

CHAPTER FIVE
How to Make Kimchi 25

CHAPTER SIX
How to Make Fermented Salsa 28

CHAPTER SEVEN
Recipes Using Fermented Vegetables 30
    Sauerkraut 30
        Reuben Sandwich 30
        Kapustnyak (Sauerkraut soup) 32
        Braised Sauerkraut 33
        Pork Chops with Sauerkraut and Apples 35
        Turkey Kielbasa and Sauerkraut 36
        Crockpot Sausage with Potatoes and Sauerkraut 37
    Pickles 38
        Potato Salad 38
        Black Bean Tacos 39
        Italian Antipasto Platter 40
        Black Bean Burgers 41
        Pickle Slaw Burgers 42
        Pickled Salmon 43
        Tuna Salad 44
    Kimchi 45
        Kimchi Fried Rice 45
        Jjigae (Kimchi stew) 47
        Roasted Chicken and Potatoes 48

Kimchi Vegetable Stew *49*
Kimchi Fried Rice with Squid and Poached Egg *50*
Spicy Kimchi and Chicken Noodles *51*
Stir-Fry with Brown Rice *52*
Salsa *53*
Baked Salsa Chicken *53*
Roasted Sweet Potatoes with Poached Eggs *54*
Cod with Lime and Salsa *55*
Salsa Meatloaf *56*
Breakfast Burrito *57*
Tropical Chicken Bowl *58*
Bean Soup with Salsa *59*

Conclusion **60**

Introduction

Hundreds of years ago, there were no refrigerators. It was invented in the 1800s as a way of putting food on ice. Before refrigeration, food was saved in other ways. Around the world, different cultures used various methods for food preservation.

Curing is one of the most common ancient methods, though it isn't used as much today outside of smoked salmon and case meats (like ham, hotdogs, and bacon). To cure something is to use salt or smoke to inhibit the growth of bacteria and keep food longer.

Another form of food preservation was sugaring, which also prevented the growth of bacteria and provided a way to store fruits longer. Sugaring is still used today in canned fruits, jams, and jellies. Sugaring doesn't last as long as curing, and it can initiate the process of fermentation, the topic of this book.

Fermentation is food preservation without refrigeration. In the U.S, most of us understand that the refrigerator is the best method of keeping food safe to consume. This is because of the constant reminders from a variety of sources that anything out of the refrigerator will spoil and cause sickness. While this is true for many foods, it's not true for everything.

The fermentation process doesn't require refrigeration, yet the food stays safe. Some examples of fermented foods you have probably eaten include pickled vegetables, such as cucumbers or onions, sauerkraut, kimchi, yogurt, and perhaps surprisingly, most alcohol.

In this book, we're going to talk about fermentation. We'll explore the why's and the how's of the fermentation process. Then we'll get into different vegetables that you can ferment in your home and recipes that you can use those fermented vegetables in.

Fermentation isn't something you want to experiment with unless you've had some experience. So make sure you follow the steps in this book to have a safe and delicious outcome. Let's get started.

CHAPTER ONE

Why Ferment Vegetables: Understanding Health Benefits

If you don't have a lot of experience with fermentation, you might be wondering what it is exactly. The Food and Agriculture Organization of the United Nations defines the process as a slow decomposition of organic materials of plant or animal origins. The decomposition is brought on by microorganisms and enzymes. It doesn't mean that the food is going bad or turning rotten. It simply means that the substance of the food is changing, due to the fermentation process.

Vegetables are low in acid, unlike fruits. This can create a situation where the veggies are more likely to deteriorate before being eaten or processed, so fermentation helps them stick around a little longer. Fermenting vegetables requires the enzymes and microorganisms to raise the level of acidity in the food, and that's done by pickling, salting, or drying them out. Natural bacteria are put to work, and they increase the amount of lactic acid while breaking down the sugar and starch in vegetables.

A History Lesson

Fermentation was originally used as a way to preserve food. Without the benefit of cold storage, ancient civilizations needed to keep the food they harvested for as long as possible. Anthropologists tell us that the first fermented foods humans consumed were likely fruits. Once alcohol was discovered as a way to preserve food, bread making and fermentation really gained popularity. The first place that vegetables were fermented was probably China. They developed molds that were used to keep vegetables from rotting too soon to be enjoyed.

The process of fermenting food has undergone many changes throughout cultures and historical periods. However, it has primarily been passed down from generation to generation and from older family members to younger ones. Cooking and food preparation are an important part of community and family bonds. So while there might not be history books written about food fermentation, it's a skill and a process that has been shared over the last hundreds and even thousands of years. It is traditional.

The Reasoning Behind Fermentation

Why should we ferment vegetables? You should ferment vegetables because they're delicious. That's my first argument, although maybe it's not the reason why you started reading this book. Personally, the taste factor is probably my only reason for fermenting. Fermenting adds a tremendous amount of flavor to our foods and cooking. In fact, in many countries, fermented foods are often served as a side dish to add flavor to other foods or cleanse the palate. Kimchi, for example, is a staple in most Korean households and is often served as a side. Miso, in Japan, is used to flavor many different foods, from soups to meats. Pickles in the U.S. and Europe are used to add taste and texture to meat products. And don't get me started on the amazing taste of cheese and its use worldwide. While fermented products can be a side dish, they can also be a main dish in the case of many fermented meats, curries, or yogurt.

Another reason to ferment vegetables is to preserve your vegetable harvest, if that's what you do, or to preserve a large number of vegetables from the store. If you grow your own vegetables or simply love cabbage and buy it in bulk, fermenting is a great way to make use of your extra produce.

So taste and storage are two key reasons people ferment foods, but they also do it for health benefits.

Health Benefits

Eating fermented vegetables can help with weight loss, better gut health, easier digestion, improved mood, and an overall healthier physical and mental environment for your body and mind. One of the most important ingredients in fermented vegetables is probiotics. These probiotics plant beneficial bacteria into the digestive system and keep everything balanced internally.

A healthy ecosystem of probiotics in your gut can prevent and possibly reverse the onset of chronic diseases and other ailments. Probiotics will help your body store the things it needs and flush out the things it doesn't. They assist in building stronger immunity, which will keep you healthier overall. You'll also benefit from better bowel health, improved digestion, and a clean, clear intestinal tract. Many recent studies have called the gut a "second brain," meaning it needs just as much care and attention as the brain in your head. Probiotics that come from fermented vegetables can help.

When you eat fermented vegetables, you also do a better job of absorbing the vitamins and minerals you need. The digestive enzymes in those fermented foods will go to work and help you absorb the necessary nutrients that keep you in good shape.

A body that is better balanced will function better. If you're trying to lose weight, you know you need to eat more vegetables and less starchy foods and sugar-filled products. Fresh veggies are great, and fermented veggies can also help you flush out excess water and toxins that you might be holding on to. Eating this way will improve your chances of slimming down and help you learn to eat better in general.

Oh! One last important note, eat fermented foods in moderation, just like you would with other foods. Too many, and you'll be adding a lot of salt or acid (depending on the fermentation process) to your diet. So make sure your vegetable intake is diversified (fresh vs. fermented vs. canned etc.). This chapter talked about the 'whys' of fermenting. The following chapters will talk about the 'hows.'

CHAPTER TWO

How to Ferment Vegetables at Home

It's one thing to be on board with the health benefits of eating fermented vegetables. However, it's another thing entirely to set about fermenting them on your own. Don't worry. If you're wondering how to ferment vegetables, it's completely manageable. You'll be surprised at how little is required. Fermenting at home can be healthy and fun. There are just a few specifics you need to get straight when you're learning how to ferment vegetables yourself.

Most people find that fermented vegetables have a tangy or sour taste. Think of pickles or sauerkraut. That taste comes from the ability of lactic acid to break down sugar and starch in the vegetables. That's what you're trying to achieve.

The Factors

Water

Water is one of the first ingredients for your product, besides the vegetables, of course. The water you choose can impact the fermentation process. If you live in an area where the city provides water, it probably has many microbe-killing chemicals like chlorine and fluoride. While these are good for drinking, they're not great for fermentation. Remember, with fermentation, we're trying to increase microbe activity, so chlorine and fluoride can kill them off. If you use city water, you can purchase distilled water (water without chemicals or minerals) or process your tap water. To prepare tap water, boil it on the stove to remove the chlorine, though it won't remove other chemicals.

If you have well water, you probably won't have any chemicals in your water, but it's a good idea to get it tested anyway. I currently live with well water, and we get it tested annually for about $50 from the local university cooperative extension. Well water and spring water are both higher in minerals, which can work for some fermentation processes and not for others. That's more of a "test as you go" scenario since we each live in different areas and have different minerals in our water.

When using water, you'll add ingredients like salt or spices to change the characteristics of water and improve the development of the good bacteria in your fermenting process. This is called brine. Your brine will either use salt or starter cultures.

Salt

Salt is a necessary ingredient when you're fermenting your own veggies. Salt helps to create the environment that's just right for fermentation. It allows microorganisms to develop and grow. It protects your vegetables against the development of harmful bacteria while allowing the healthy bacteria to thrive.

You can use salt in a couple of different ways when you're fermenting your food. Simply tossing your vegetables in a good quantity of salt will draw water out of the veggies, preparing them to ferment properly. Use at least one tablespoon of salt for every pound of vegetables you want to ferment. You can also create a brine. In this process, the vegetables are soaked in the liquid before they ferment. Salt creates a stable and productive environment for your food.

Cultures

You can add fermentation cultures to improve fermentation or the flavor of fermented vegetables. You can purchase commercially made starter cultures to begin your fermentation process. Choose different ones for different products. For example, if you're making yogurt or kefir, make sure that you choose a lactic culture starter. When you use the recipes from this book, choose a vegetable starter.

If using a commercial starter isn't for you, there's a great alternative. Once you've finished making your first batch of fermented vegetables, save some brine. This brine is teeming with microbes that can be used to start a new batch. You'll need about ¼ cup of brine for each quart of new vegetables.

Creating the Conditions

Food safety needs to be your primary concern when fermenting your own vegetables. Make sure you are creating conditions that are safe, edible, and productive. If anything looks, smells, or tastes off—don't eat it. When you start with good, healthy vegetables that have not been exposed to bacteria such as E. coli or salmonella, you're in good shape. There are a few specific things to pay attention to as you set up your own fermenting system.

Temperature is important. Ideally, your fermentation process will take place between 60 degrees and 75 degrees. If you allow the temperature to slip below 60, the vegetables are unlikely to ferment at all. If the temperature goes higher than 75, the problem is that the food will become soft and too limp to enjoy. It might taste spoiled. If you're fermenting something like sauerkraut, the ideal temperature is between 70 and 75 degrees. You'll have a fully fermented food product in just a few weeks.

When you reach the correct temperature of between 60 and 75 degrees, the harmful bacteria and potential pathogens will be destroyed by the healthy bacteria and the enzymes that you want to keep in your food. The right temperature will also keep the vegetables from rotting.

Many people who ferment their food like to store the containers in a dark place or cover them with cloth to prevent light from affecting the food. The idea behind keeping the fermentation process dark is that you'll be able to preserve more of the Vitamin C in your vegetables this way. You never want to expose your vegetables to direct sunlight. Too much light will destroy the lactic bacteria, which will corrupt your entire process. So, keep the fermenting vegetables in a dry, dark place that hovers between 60 degrees and 75 degrees.

You'll also need to keep your container in which you are fermenting free of oxygen. For example, make sure the lid is on tight if you're using a mason jar to ferment cucumbers, broccoli, or cabbage. There could be a build-up of gas a few days after fermentation starts, in which case you'll need to loosen the lid for a few seconds to allow the oxygen and carbon dioxide to escape. Lactic acid bacteria do not need oxygen to survive, and you don't want mold to develop.

Equipment

Containers

You have a few options when it comes to what you'll use to ferment your vegetables. There are specialty ceramic containers used to ferment foods, but any glass container that's high quality and sturdy will work. Try to avoid using a plastic container as the fermentation process can be fairly abrasive, and you don't want chemicals from the plastic leaching into your fermented food.

Make sure you don't use metal because the acid will corrode it. You also don't want any dents, scratches, or other anomalies to the container that will allow bad bacteria or other substances to creep in. A simple mason jar is one of the easiest containers to use.

If you use canning jars that come with metal lids, you'll want to avoid the metal corroding from the acid in the jar. As the bacteria in the jar change during the fermenting process, the brine will often become acidic and can eat away at the metal lids of jars. To avoid this, place a barrier like wax paper between the lid and the fermenting vegetables, or replace the lid with a glass or plastic one.

As long as you have your container, everything can be done in your kitchen. There are elaborate vessels and crocks available, but purchasing those is not necessary.

Weights and a Thermometer

Since fermentation requires the vegetables to be submerged in water, you want to make sure they stay submerged. If you've made a vegetable soup, you probably know that the vegetables don't want to stay down. They float to the top of any liquid because of the amount of air in their cells. To combat this, you'll need to push the vegetables down with a press.

A press can be a pestle, mortar, or anything else that fits into your jar (like a potato masher) and pushes the ingredients into the jar. This will help release their juices but also remove some of the air.

Since vegetables will want to float up, even after pressing them, you'll want to weigh them down. You can purchase specially made fermenting weights for a very low price, or you can use pie weights in a bag. You can also use just a large cabbage leaf if you're making a cabbage-based recipe. Any large pieces of vegetables can weigh down smaller pieces. If you have a large crock, you can place a plate that fits in and weigh it down with a bottle of water. You just want to make sure that your vegetables stay submerged, or else it will encourage mold growth.

Finally, depending on the temperature of your house and the season, you may want to check the temperature of your vegetables as you go along. Remember from the discussion earlier that temperature is important for the fermentation process. An instant-read thermometer is a good choice, although you can also use a dial thermometer.

Preparing and Storing the Food

Simply slice, chop, or cube the vegetables you want to ferment. You can use anything you like, such as onions, cucumbers, cabbage, broccoli, carrots, cauliflower, asparagus, and eggplant. The veggies should be clean and fresh and cut into uniform sizes that will fit into the container you've chosen. Depending on what you're fermenting and the recipe you're using, all you have to do is cover the vegetables with water, salt, and perhaps some herbs and spices.

You'll know the vegetables are fermenting because you'll see some bubbles begin to form. Tasting the veggies is the best way to determine whether the fermentation process is finished. Start tasting them after a week and remember that the longer they ferment, the stronger the flavor will become.

You'll know the fermentation is done when the product tastes good to you or whoever else will be eating it. The taste will change many times during the process, so tasting along the way can help you find what tastes you prefer. Once you've reached a flavor you like, you can move the fermented vegetables into cold storage.

After fermentation, store your mix in the refrigerator. You can also store it in a cool dark cellar, basement, or cold pantry. It will continue to ferment but at a much slower rate. Remember that air will lead to spoilage, so if there's a lot of air in the storage container, move the mix into a smaller container. Fermented vegetables can be enjoyed for weeks and even months but follow the same taste testing rules below to determine if your food is still good after it's been stored.

If you want to, you can process your fermented vegetables (canning) for a much longer shelf life at room temperature. Canning is an exact process, so if this is how you want to store your fermented vegetables, follow clear and accurate recipes. It can be a little daunting the first time you try it, but as a seasoned canner, I guarantee it's much easier than it looks, and you'll have a year to enjoy your food before worrying about spoilage. You can find some good canning tips at the National Center for Home Food Preservation website. They have a complete publication on how to can fermented food.

Precautions and Troubleshooting

Test your mix often. It shouldn't smell bad. If it does, then throw it out. If it smells okay, then taste it. If it smells sour but still good, then taste it. If anything looks or tastes off—don't eat it. Tasting along the way can help you determine how the process is going.

Fermenting can often be a trial and error process. You might notice some mold, which means oxygen has crept in. The vegetables could taste terrible, in which case you need to adjust the length of time they ferment or the temperature at which they are stored. You might also notice that the brine you are fermenting your vegetables in begins to overflow or push against your lid. You'll need to release some of that pressure and possibly remove some vegetables if your container is too crowded.

If you notice a white foam developing on your vegetables, don't panic. If it's not fuzzy, then it's not mold. It could be yeast that is perfectly healthy. Keep it. What you don't want to see are insects. Remember that fermented food is live food. Some insects that were on the vegetables unbeknownst to you could have left some eggs on that food, and those eggs can hatch in the environment you've created. Compost that batch and start over.

Knowing how to ferment vegetables on your own can open up a new world of possibilities for you and your kitchen. It's not hard or frightening, and if you're willing to try it a few times, you will likely develop a system that works well and delivers delicious, healthy foods filled with probiotics and gut-gorgeous bacteria. Try the recipes in this book, and don't be afraid to get creative on your own.

CHAPTER THREE

How to Make Sauerkraut

Sauerkraut is probably one of the most familiar fermented foods. It's often an accompaniment to German food, but it is good with many meals. Sauerkraut ferments cabbage with occasional other vegetables added.

Basic Sauerkraut Recipe

Ingredients:
1 head of green cabbage
1½ tablespoons of salt
1 sharp knife
1 mason jar with airtight lid

Directions:
1. Wash and dry the mason jar. For the good bacteria to take over any potential bad bacteria, a pristine environment is necessary.
2. Wash and dry the cabbage. Discard any limp or hanging outer leaves.
3. Keep one large leaf of cabbage to the side. Then, slice and chop the cabbage into thin strips. You ultimately want a pile of thin ribbons that are more or less uniform in size.
4. Put the cabbage into a large bowl and sprinkle the salt over it. After allowing it to rest for a couple of minutes, start massaging the salt into the cabbage by hand (make sure those hands are clean). Squeeze the cabbage as you work the salt into it. After about 10 minutes, you'll notice the cabbage is becoming wet and soft.
5. Pack the cabbage into the mason jar. Take one handful at a time and press the vegetables firmly into the bottom of the jar. Once

you get to the top of your jar, take the leaf you set aside and place it over the shredded cabbage. This will keep the shredded pieces in place. It's very important for the cabbage to remain submerged in the liquid it produces for the fermentation process to work properly.

6. Tighten the lid over the jar and store it in a cool, dark, and dry location. Ideally, you'll find a spot with a temperature between 65 and 70 degrees.

7. Ferment the sauerkraut for three to five days. If you notice bubbles forming at the top of the jar, open the lid and allow the gas that's building up to escape.

8. Taste your sauerkraut. The longer you let it ferment, the stronger the taste will become. You can refrigerate it, and the sauerkraut will keep for several months.

Above is a simple explanation for how to make sauerkraut. Here are a couple of variations you can try.

Variation Recipes

Carrot Kraut

Most sauerkrauts are all about the cabbage, but this variation includes carrots for a slightly sweeter taste. It's a good kraut option if you have children in the house who will eat it. This recipe is a dry salting method and doesn't require a brine.

Ingredients:
1 small cabbage, shredded
3 large carrots, shredded
1 tablespoon sea salt

Directions:
1. Place all the ingredients in a bowl and mix. You can use your press or pestle to mash the ingredients a bit. Set the bowl aside for about 30 minutes for the vegetable liquid to seep.
2. Place the mixture into your fermentation jar, and make sure all pieces are under the liquid. You can use a weight to keep them down. Cover the jar (check the section on Precautions and Troubleshooting in Chapter 2).
3. Process the fermentation until it reaches your preferred texture and taste, then move to cold storage.

Salt-free Kraut

Using salt in sauerkraut is essential to ensure a crispy vegetable. However, if you're trying to avoid salt, you can use this recipe as an alternative. Just keep in mind that the cabbage won't be as crisp, and there might be mold growth since there isn't any salt to inhibit mold.

Keep a close eye on it. Compost that batch and start over if you see mold growing.

Ingredients:
5 lbs cabbage, shredded
1 tablespoon celery seeds
1 tablespoon peppercorns
1 tablespoon caraway seeds
1 tablespoon dill seeds
Distilled water

Directions:

1. Grind all of the spices. Then place all the ingredients, except water, in a bowl and mix. You can use your press or pestle to mash the ingredients a bit.

2. Place the mixture into your fermentation jar, and pour over enough water to cover the cabbage. Make sure all pieces are under the liquid. You can use a weight to keep them down. Cover the jar.

3. Process the fermentation for five days and continue until it reaches your preferred texture and taste, then move to cold storage.

CHAPTER FOUR

How to Make Pickles and Relishes

There's so much that can be done with pickles. When we think of pickles, we typically think about cucumbers submerged in a tangy, flavorful brine. However, pickles can be made from many vegetables, not just cucumbers. Some of my personal favorites are onions, watermelon rind, and beets.

To pickle any vegetable, you want to make sure that the pickles will still be crisp after fermentation. You know the difference between the pickles you buy in a grocery store in the ketchup aisle versus those bought in the deli section. The ones that have been cold processed are delicious and nutritious. The ones in the aisle are soggy and not nearly as delicious. You want to do the same with your pickling at home. So make pickles at a cooler temperature.

Basic pickles are pretty straightforward. You combine the vegetable of choice (whole or sliced) with spices and brine. Your brine can be made with salt for natural fermentation, or you can add a commercial culture product to the brine. Just follow the directions on the box of culture starter you purchase. For cucumber pickles, some seasoning choices are dill weed, garlic, mustard seeds, and peppercorns. You can mess around with the spices to fit your tastes. Other types of pickled vegetables can use different seasonings. You don't have to grind any of the seasonings, and you can use fresh ones if you have that option.

Here are some great pickling recipes:

Cucumber Pickles

This is just a basic recipe, but you can adapt it to fit your taste.
Ingredients:

1 lb pickling cucumbers, sliced
1½ tablespoons sea salt
¾ cup distilled water
Spices like dill seeds and mustard seeds
2 garlic cloves, minced

Directions:

1. In a bowl, combine the water and salt, stirring until the salt dissolves.

2. Place the cucumber slices and spices into a fermentation jar. You can alternate layers, adding spices throughout the mix. Pour the brine over the cucumbers and make sure all pieces are under the liquid. You can use a weight to keep them down.

3. Secure the top of the jar with a lid. You can also use a clean cloth then put a fitted plate on top of the jar. Apply some weight to the plate, so air doesn't get into the jar and cause mold.

4. Store the jar in a cool, dark place. The fermenting process will begin immediately, and you'll have crispy sour pickles in a matter of days. Depending on the temperature, the amount of time you need to ferment the pickles fully will be between two and four weeks. Keep the pickles for months in the fridge and enjoy them as snacks and sides.

Pickled Watermelon Rind

Watermelon rind might sound like a strange thing to pickle, but hear me out. Watermelon rind is similar to cucumbers in flavor and texture and makes the perfect pickling ingredient. Try it to see if you agree.

Ingredients:

Rind of 1 watermelon, dark green skin and pink flesh removed, cut into chunks or slices

2 tablespoons sea salt

4 cups distilled water

Spices like coriander and peppercorns (optional).

Directions:

1. In a bowl, combine the water and salt, stirring until the salt dissolves.

2. Place the watermelon rind and spices into a fermentation jar. You can alternate layers, adding spices throughout the mix. Pour the

brine over the rind and make sure all pieces are under the liquid. You can use a weight to keep them down.

3. Cover the jar and store it in a cool, dark place.

4. Process the fermentation until it reaches your preferred texture and taste, then move to cold storage.

Pickled Onions

Pickled onions are a great addition to heavy meals. Eat them alongside pot roast, burgers, or any healthy meat product. They're also great on sandwiches for a boost of flavor.

Ingredients:
2 cups red onions, sliced, or whole pearl onions
1 tablespoon sea salt
2 cups distilled water
Spices like coriander, mustard, and peppercorns (optional)

Directions:
1. In a bowl, combine the water and salt, stirring until the salt dissolves.

2. Place the onions and spices into a fermentation jar. You can alternate layers, adding spices throughout the mix. Pour the brine over the onions and make sure all pieces are under the liquid. You can use a weight to keep them down.

3. Cover the jar and store it in a cool, dark place.

4. Process the fermentation until it reaches your preferred texture and taste, then move to cold storage.

Relishes

Relishes make the perfect condiment to a meal. Unlike pickles or sauerkraut, relishes are often a combination of several different vegetables or fruits with spices. They don't usually require brine because they are more sauce-like. You will, however, still use salt. Relishes are a good option for canning, so if you want to save your fermentation longer, consider canning the relish in small canning jars.

A basic relish recipe is 4 cups of mixed, grated, or chopped vegetables or fruit (cranberries and apples, beets and carrots, corn and pepper, etc.), season to taste, salt, and an added culture. You'll process it based on the culture instructions on the box. You'll only process it for a few days, less than a week, and once it's finished, it will only keep for a couple of weeks. If you want a specific recipe, here's one you can try:

Squash Relish

This recipe is very savory and a great condiment. It's also spicy, so adjust the spice as you like.

Ingredients:
3 cups summer squash, shredded
½ cup onion, chopped
Jalapeno pepper, seeded and chopped (adjust to taste)
1 bell pepper, minced
3 garlic cloves, minced
¼ teaspoon red pepper flakes
½ tablespoon sea salt
¼ cup distilled water
Black peppercorns

Directions:
1. Place all the ingredients in a bowl and mix. You can use your press or pestle to mash the ingredients a bit.
2. Place the mixture into your fermentation jar, and make sure everything is pressed down. You want to have about 1-inch of space between the relish and the rim of the jar.
3. Cover the jar and store it in a cool, dark place.

4. Process the fermentation for 2–3 days, then move to cold storage. Unlike other types of fermenting, relishes will only last for a couple of weeks.

CHAPTER FIVE

How to Make Kimchi

Kimchi is a beautiful dish. It's spicy, briny, and crisp. It's the perfect accompaniment to rice or stir fry dishes. Kimchi is originally from Korea. Like sauerkraut, it's a combination of vegetables like cabbage or radishes, with salt. However, they differ after that. Kimchi is spiced with traditional Korean spices and often has fish sauce added.

There are many variations, but typically the main vegetable is napa cabbage or daikon radish. If you've never had daikon radish, it's a very mild, slightly soft type of radish. This is seasoned with chili peppers, ginger, onions, and additional ingredients. It's easy to make at home. I'm going to share the recipe my college roommate taught me. She made it nearly every week when we were in school, kept it under the kitchen sink, and I swear it started my love of fermented foods.

The following recipe makes a pretty big batch. You can increase or decrease it as you desire. You'll also need a pair of disposable kitchen gloves to mix everything. It may be hard to find some of the ingredients in your local grocery store, but you can find many of these ingredients in an Asian market in your area or even online. Kimchi is a much longer process than some of the other recipes in this book. There are also a lot of spices in it, so be prepared for that, and do not under any circumstances touch your eyes after touching the spices. I learned that the hard way the first time I made it. The gloves are crucial.

Ingredients:

2 heads napa cabbage, chopped into 2-inch pieces and thoroughly washed

1 cup sea salt

1½ cups distilled water
¼ cup sweet rice powder
¼ cup sugar
1-inch piece ginger, sliced
one whole head garlic, peeled
¼ cup onion, sliced
¼ cup fish sauce (skip this if you are vegan)
2 cup daikon radish, diced
1 bunch scallions, cut into small pieces
1½ cups gochugaru (Korean red pepper powder)
⅓ cup salted shrimp, drained and finely chopped into a paste (Also skip this if you're a vegan)

Directions:

1. In a large bowl, place the cabbage and salt in alternating layers. Place it to the side for about an hour, then mix. Let it sit again for another hour, then give it a good rinse. The cabbage should be wilted and have expelled some water. Drain the cabbage and set it aside.

2. In a saucepan, add water and sweet rice powder, whisking to incorporate. Don't stop whisking. Bring to a gentle simmer and cook until it's thick. Add sugar, continue cooking for another minute, and then remove from the heat. Let it cool.

3. In a blender, add ginger, garlic, onions, and fish sauce, blending until smooth.

4. Now you're ready to make the seasoning. Add the rice mixture, ginger mixture, daikon, scallions, gochugaru, and shrimp together. Mix well with your hands.

5. Add the seasoning to the cabbage and mix thoroughly.

6. Pack this mixture into your fermenting jars or crock. Using your press, push all the ingredients down in the jar, removing as much air as possible. You can press some plastic wrap directly on top of the vegetables since there isn't a liquid brine to cover them.

7. Cover the jar and store your kimchi in a cool, dark place where the temperature will be no lower than 60 degrees and no higher than 75 degrees.

8. If you see bubbles float to the top of the jar, simply unscrew the lid and allow some of the gas to escape. Put the lid back on securely and allow it to continue fermenting.

9. After about three days, taste the kimchi. Once you get it to the desired balance of flavors, store it in the refrigerator and enjoy it for several weeks.

CHAPTER SIX

How to Make Fermented Salsa

Tomatoes are one of the healthiest foods you can eat. In their fresh, raw form, they are filled with vitamins, minerals, and antioxidants to help you fight off diseases. Fermenting tomatoes will allow you to harness all that goodness and add some bonus health benefits. You get the probiotics present in fermented foods when you learn to make fermented salsa. The instructions here are for half a gallon of salsa. You'll find it's one of the tastiest salsas you've ever had, and you can enjoy it on chips, raw veggies, or on top of meat, fish, and chicken.

Ingredients:
2 or 3 small glass canning jars with lids
2 lbs fresh tomatoes, chopped
1 red onion, chopped
1 red bell pepper, chopped
1 green bell pepper, chopped
1 orange bell pepper, chopped
5 garlic cloves, peeled
½ cup whole cilantro leaves
2 limes, juiced
1 tablespoon sea salt
½ teaspoon chili powder
½ cup whey

Directions:
1. Place all the ingredients in a bowl and mix. You can use your press or pestle to mash the ingredients a bit. Set the bowl aside for about 30 minutes for the vegetable liquid to start seeping.

2. Transfer the mixture to the jars, and make sure all pieces are under the liquid (add some water if you need to). You can use a weight to keep them down.

3. Cover the jars and store them in a cool, dark place.

4. Process the fermentation for two days or until it reaches your preferred texture and taste, then move to cold storage.

Everyone has different tastes when it comes to salsa. If you like yours less spicy, cut down to ¼ teaspoon of the chili powder. If you don't like onion, leave it out. You can adjust these ingredients to what you prefer in your favorite tomato-based topping. The whey is present to help break down and ferment the tomatoes; if you're intolerant to whey, consider making a brine or using other already-fermented liquids.

CHAPTER SEVEN

Recipes Using Fermented Vegetables

Now that you know how to ferment vegetables, you'll be looking for recipes to incorporate those vegetables into meals. Try the recipes below. You'll find that the fermented veggies complement the other food on your plate and leave you feeling satisfied. They also taste great, and you know they're contributing to the healthy bacteria ecosystem in your digestive and intestinal tracts.

Sauerkraut

The sauerkraut recipes here give you a variety of options. The first is a sandwich (the best sandwich in my humble opinion), the second a farmer's soup, the third a delicately braised stew, and the fourth a pork chop. All these recipes are delicious and the perfect way to use your sauerkraut.

Reuben Sandwich

Let's start with a quintessential sauerkraut recipe. Everyone knows how popular Reubens are, and sauerkraut is probably the best part. You can always make it in a panini press if you have one, but otherwise, a skillet on the stove works just fine. Set up the sandwich in a cold skillet, so you don't have to juggle a full sandwich into a pan.

Makes 1 serving

Ingredients:
2 slices rye or pumpernickel bread
2 teaspoons butter, softened, not melted

2 tablespoons Russian dressing (purchase or make your own)

¼ cup sauerkraut, well-drained (squeeze out the liquid if you can).

2 oz Swiss cheese, thinly sliced

¼ lb corned beef, thinly sliced.

Directions:

1. On one side of each slice of your bread, spread butter from edge to edge. Then place one slice in a cold skillet, butter-side down. Spread the dressing on the one slice in the skillet, then add the sauerkraut.

2. Add the cheese on top of the sauerkraut, followed by the corned beef.

3. On the second slice, spread the remaining dressing on the dry side of the bread. Place it, with the buttered side up, on top of the sandwich.

4. Place the skillet on the stove and turn to medium-low heat. Grill the sandwich in the pan, pressing it down like you would a grilled cheese sandwich. Continue cooking until the bottom is crisp, then flip the sandwich, so the un-grilled slice is now directly on the pan.

5. You'll want to press the sandwich again. You can use a spatula, but you can also use a plate so that it's evenly pressed. Grill until the second side is crisp.

6. Serve and enjoy.

Kapustnyak (Sauerkraut soup)

This soup is the perfect medium for sauerkraut. It's a hearty, delicious, and warming soup popular in Ukraine and Poland. Enjoy!

Makes 8 servings

Ingredients:

1 tablespoon olive oil
½ lb bacon, chopped
1 stalk celery, finely diced
1 onion, finely diced
2 carrots, thinly sliced
1 lb potatoes, peeled and sliced into ¼ inch pieces
¼ cup quinoa, rinsed
2–3 cups sauerkraut
8 cups chicken broth, low sodium
2 cups water, or a little less
15 oz canned white beans
Salt and pepper to taste

Directions:

1. Drain the fermented sauerkraut. You can soak it in water and rinse if it has a very strong taste, but that's your choice.

2. In a Dutch oven, heat 1 tablespoon of oil. Add the bacon and sauté until browned. Remove from the oil (leave the oil in the pot).

3. Add the celery, onions, and carrots. Sauté on low heat, sweating the onions, but not browning them. Cook for about 5 minutes.

4. Add potatoes, quinoa, broth, and water to the pot. Bring the pot to a boil and then reduce the heat to a simmer. Cook for about 15 minutes.

5. Add the sauerkraut, bacon, and beans. Continue cooking until the potatoes are cooked through. Season the soup to taste and serve.

Braised Sauerkraut

This is a dish where sauerkraut plays the key role. It's delicious and makes a perfect main dish. You can serve it with some roasted potatoes or other starchy vegetables.

Makes 8 servings

Ingredients:

3 lbs pork roast
2 lbs sauerkraut
½ lb bacon, chopped into small pieces
1 cup carrots, sliced thinly
2 cups onions, sliced
2 tablespoons butter
4 sprigs parsley
1 bay leaf
6 peppercorns
¼ cup gin
1 cup sparkling wine
3 cups chicken stock

Directions:

1. Preheat your oven to 325°F.
2. Drain the fermented sauerkraut. You can soak it in water if it has a very strong taste, but that's your choice.
3. In a Dutch oven, cook the bacon, carrots, and onions in butter. Cook at low heat, sweating the onions without browning them. Add the sauerkraut and mix well. Then cover and cook on low for 10 minutes.
4. Add the spices, wine, gin, and stock until the liquid covers the sauerkraut. Season with salt and pepper, then increase the heat and bring the mix to a simmer.
5. Cut some parchment paper to fit the inside of the pan, just in a circle, and butter one side. Place the buttered side down on top of

the kraut. Then cover the Dutch oven and set it in the oven. Cook for 3½ hours.

4. In the meantime, brown the pork roast on all sides. After the kraut dish has been simmering for 3 hours, add the meat and bury it within the sauerkraut. Continue to braise in the oven for another 1½ hours.

5. Serve and enjoy. It's particularly delicious in winter.

Pork Chops with Sauerkraut and Apples

Makes 4 servings

Ingredients:
4 pork chops, bone-in
4 cups sauerkraut
2 tablespoons olive oil
2 apples, peeled and sliced
1 tablespoon butter
1 tablespoon brown sugar
3 teaspoons dried rosemary
Salt and pepper

Directions:
1. Preheat the oven to 375°F.
2. In a large skillet, heat the olive oil and add the pork chops. Sprinkle the salt, pepper, and rosemary on the meat and cook until they are brown; 5 minutes on the first side and 3 minutes on the next.
3. Layer the bottom of a baking dish with the sauerkraut and place the pork chops on top. Cook in the oven for 30–40 minutes, until pork is done.
4. Meanwhile, in a small saucepan, melt the butter and stir in the brown sugar. Add the apple slices and toss.

Turkey Kielbasa and Sauerkraut

Makes 4 servings

Ingredients:
1 lb turkey kielbasa
2 pints sauerkraut
1 tablespoon caraway seeds
2 tablespoons olive oil
2 cups black beans, rinsed

Directions:

1. In a skillet, heat the olive oil. Poke fork holes into the kielbasa links and cook them in the oil over medium-high heat until they brown on the outside, for about five minutes.

2. Remove the kielbasa and allow it to cool for three minutes. While it's cooling, add the sauerkraut and beans to the pan and stir in the caraway seeds.

3. Slice the kielbasa into one-inch pieces and return it to the pan.

4. Continue to cook all the ingredients together until the meat is cooked all the way through.

Crockpot Sausage with Potatoes and Sauerkraut

Makes 4 servings

Ingredients:

1½ lbs potatoes
2 cups sauerkraut
1 small onion, peeled and sliced
½ cup chicken broth
¼ cup white wine
1 teaspoon caraway seeds
Some freshly chopped parsley
1½ lbs bratwurst links
½ teaspoon salt
1 teaspoon olive oil
½ teaspoon pepper

Directions:

1. Wash the potatoes thoroughly and peel them. Dice using a sharp kitchen knife.
2. Heat the olive oil in a large pan over medium-high heat.
3. Add sliced onions and sauté for a couple of minutes until slightly brown.
4. Throw in the diced potatoes and sauerkraut and stir for 2 minutes.
5. Sprinkle salt, pepper, and caraway seeds and mix well using a spoon.
6. Add the bratwurst, chicken broth, and wine, and give it a stir again.
7. Transfer the mixture to your slow cooker. Cook the mixture for about 7–8 hours on low, or 5 hours on high.
8. Sprinkle chopped parsley leaves on top before serving.

Pickles

For most of us, pickles are a side or an addition to a sandwich. In the seven recipes here, pickles are added for flavor. The first is a potato salad, a great dish to bring to a BBQ. The second dish is tacos with pickled onions as a topping. The third is a delicious Italian antipasto platter.

Potato Salad

In many potato salad recipes, you'll use a sweet pickle. If you've made a sweet pickle, then, of course, use it. This recipe is for a more savory pickle. This potato salad takes advantage of that flavor to give you a potato salad with a kick.

Makes 12 servings

Ingredients:

3 lbs red potatoes, skinned, cooked, and cooled
1 cup dill pickles, chopped
1½ cups celery, diced
6 hard-boiled eggs, peeled and chopped
1¼ cups mayonnaise
3 tablespoons white onion, finely minced
4 tablespoons pickle juice (from your fermented pickles)
1 tablespoon white vinegar
1½ tablespoons Dijon mustard
4 tablespoons fresh dill, minced
Salt and pepper to taste

Directions:

1. In a bowl, mix together the mayo, onion, pickle juice, vinegar, mustard, and dill. Mix well.

2. Add the rest of the ingredients. Mash some of the potatoes, but leave the rest as is.

3. Serve and enjoy!

Black Bean Tacos

While you can always add pickled onions to a salad, they shine in a meat-based dish. In this recipe, pickled onions add a flair to regular tacos and help to lighten up the heaviness of the other flavors. Enjoy!

Makes 2 servings

Ingredients:

2 garlic cloves, minced
½ red onion, minced
1 jalapeno, seeded and minced
15 oz canned black beans, drained and rinsed
1½ teaspoons apple cider vinegar
½ cup basmati rice, cooked
1 teaspoon Mexican oregano
1 tablespoon chilis in adobo sauce, chopped
1 cup vegetable broth
6 corn tortillas
1 avocado, sliced
Pickled onions to taste
Fresh cilantro, finely chopped, to taste
Salt and pepper to taste

Directions:

1. In a large skillet, add garlic, onion, jalapeno, oregano, and chilis in adobo sauce. Cook until the onion is softened. Then add the black beans and mash with a fork.

2. Add the vegetable broth and vinegar. Continue cooking until the mixture has thickened, 10 minutes.

3. Warm the tortillas. Then serve with the cooked rice and the bean mix. Top with sliced avocados, pickled onions, and cilantro.

4. Serve and enjoy!

Italian Antipasto Platter

Makes 8 servings

Ingredients:
2 cups fermented pickles
1 cup Kalamata olives
1 cup Spanish olives
1 cup pickled pearl onions
1 stick pepperoni, sliced
1 cup mozzarella cheese, cubed
1 stalks celery, chopped
1 cup marinated red peppers, sliced

Directions:
1. Toss all the ingredients together in a large bowl until all the food and flavors are blended.
2. Serve in small bowls as an appetizer.

Black Bean Burgers

Makes 4 servings

Ingredients:
4 black bean burger patties
1 cup fermented pickles
4 slices provolone cheese
4 tablespoons spicy mustard
½ cup red onion, sliced
Salt and pepper

Directions:

1. Heat a grill or a grill pan and cook the black bean burgers on each side until they are done.

2. Melt a slice of cheese on top of each burger before removing them from the heat.

3. Top with mustard, red onion, and fermented pickles.

4. If you want some bread, add a bun.

5. Season with salt and pepper.

Pickle Slaw Burgers

Makes 6 servings

Ingredients:

2 lbs fresh green cabbage
1 cup carrots, peeled and sliced
¾ cup mayonnaise
2 tablespoons white wine vinegar
4 tablespoons sugar
2 tablespoons dill pickle juice
½ teaspoon salt
½ cup dill pickles
½ teaspoon cayenne pepper
6 burger buns
Fresh cherries for garnishing

Directions:

1. Wash cabbage under running water and cut it into thin slices.
2. Add cabbage to a large bowl. Combine with carrots, mayonnaise, white wine vinegar, salt, pepper, dill pickle juice, and dill pickles, and mix well with a spoon.
3. Refrigerate coleslaw for at least a couple of hours. Refrigerating it overnight will bring out more flavor.
4. Remove from fridge and mix well again.
5. Cut burger buns in half. Place coleslaw on each of the burger buns and secure with toothpicks.
6. Garnish by adding fresh cherries on top.

Pickled Salmon

Makes 4 servings

Ingredients:

4 salmon fillets
1 tablespoon black peppercorns
3 tablespoons pickled cucumber
1 teaspoon dried thyme
Some fresh parsley
1 clove
2 tablespoons sweet paprika
4 tablespoons extra virgin olive oil
2 tablespoons apple cider vinegar
2 tablespoons white wine
Sea salt to taste

Directions:

1. Using a sharp kitchen knife, cut salmon into thin strips and spread on a large plate.
2. Season with salt, thyme leaves, peppercorns, clove, cucumber pickle, and paprika and mix well. Ensure salmon is fully coated with seasoning.
3. Heat 2 tablespoons of olive oil in a large skillet over medium heat.
4. Lay salmon pieces in the skillet and sprinkle with the remaining 2 tablespoons olive oil.
5. Sprinkle with white wine vinegar.
6. Cover and cook salmon for about 10-11 minutes over low heat.
7. Garnish with fresh parsley leaves.
8. Salmon will keep in the refrigerator for up to 2 days.

Tuna Salad

Makes 4–6 servings

Ingredients:
2 cans tuna
½ cup fermented pickles
½ cup red bell pepper, diced
½ cup green bell pepper, diced
½ celery, diced
½ cup mayonnaise
1 tablespoon chopped parsley
1 tablespoon chopped thyme
1 tablespoon chopped rosemary
1 teaspoon sea salt
1 teaspoon white pepper
Crackers

Directions:
1. Combine all ingredients in a bowl except for pickles, and mix until combined.
2. Spread on crackers and top with pickles.

Kimchi

With its spicy flavors, kimchi is a perfect accent to many foods. It's usually eaten as a side dish, but in these seven recipes, kimchi is the star of the dish. These recipes are fairly easy to make, and most of the ingredients can be found in your regular grocery store.

Kimchi Fried Rice

This dish is a perfect way to use your leftover rice. It's similar to fried rice but more spicy and sour. It's a quick recipe that anyone can follow and one of my go-to recipes. Again, I learned a similar recipe from my roommate, and we ate it a lot during exams.

Makes 2 servings

Ingredients:
2 tablespoons canola oil
½ onion, diced
1 cup kimchi, chopped
3 tablespoons kimchi juice, or to taste
Any leftover meat that you want to use
2 cups white rice, cooked
2 teaspoons soy sauce
1 teaspoon sesame oil
2 eggs

Directions:
1. In a large skillet, heat the oil. You want to choose a flavorless oil like canola. Add the onion and kimchi to the pan. Cook until it's hot and the onions are soft.

2. Add the kimchi juice, meat, and rice to the pan. Continue to cook until the rice is heated through, stirring occasionally. Add the soy sauce and sesame oil, then give everything a good mix.

3. Press the rice into the pan and leave it for a bit. This will help the rice make a golden crust on the bottom. While this crisps up, fry the eggs in a separate pan. Aim for over-medium, where the yolk is still runny.

4. Serve the rice and top with the eggs. You can stir it all together or eat them as is. Enjoy!

Jjigae (Kimchi stew)

I swear that this soup probably saved me when I had strep throat. Well, not literally saved, but it was a very comforting and delicious soup. Kimchi stew is a great way to use some of your fermented kimchi. Try to wait until your kimchi is very flavorful before using it in the soup. If you want to make it even more hearty, add some Korean rice cakes into the soup in the last few minutes.

Makes 4 servings

Ingredients:

2 tablespoons sesame oil
1 lb bacon, chopped
Salt and pepper to taste
½ large yellow onion, chopped
3 cups kimchi, chopped with liquid
1 tablespoon fish sauce
5 scallions, thinly sliced

Directions:

1. In a large soup pot or Dutch oven, heat the sesame oil on medium heat. Add the bacon, season with salt, and cook until it's crispy.

2. Add the onion and kimchi to the pot, stirring it all together. Then add water to cover the mixture and bring the pot to a boil. Once it's boiling, reduce the heat to a simmer, cover the pot, and cook for about 20 minutes. You can thicken the soup with a cornstarch slurry if desired.

3. When the soup is finished cooking, add the fish sauce and scallions. Cook for 5 minutes and serve. Enjoy!

Roasted Chicken and Potatoes

This American classic gets elevated with the use of kimchi. This recipe has many parts, but it's pretty easy to put together. It's an excellent option for a weeknight dinner.

Makes 4 servings

Ingredients:

1½ lbs fingerling potatoes (baby potatoes)

4 tablespoons vegetable oil

Salt and pepper to taste

4 chicken thighs, bone-in, skin-on

2 garlic cloves, grated

2 cups kimchi

¼ cup kimchi juice

1 tablespoon rice vinegar

4 cups arugula

Directions:

1. Preheat your oven to 450°F.
2. On a large baking sheet, toss the potatoes, 1 tablespoon of the oil, salt, and pepper. Place the baking sheet in the oven and roast the potatoes until browned. This will take about 15 minutes. Stir halfway through the baking time.
3. Season the chicken with garlic, salt, and pepper. Rub the seasonings into the chicken.
4. In a large skillet, heat 1 tablespoon of oil over medium-high heat. Brown the chicken, skin-side down for about 10 minutes. Don't touch the chicken as it browns.
5. Add chicken to the baking sheet with the potatoes. Roast them together for about 20 minutes or until the chicken is finished cooking.
6. Once done, mash the potatoes, then place the kimchi over the potatoes. Roast for 5 more minutes.

7. In a bowl, combine the kimchi liquid, vinegar, and the remaining oil. Mix them all well, and then add the arugula. Mix.

8. Serve the chicken and potatoes with a side of the arugula. Enjoy!

Kimchi Vegetable Stew

Makes 4 servings

Ingredients:
1 cup kimchi
1 tablespoon olive oil
1 red onion, sliced
2 cups vegetable stock
1 teaspoon sugar
1 sweet potato, peeled and chopped into cubes
1 cup mushrooms, sliced
2 cups sliced cabbage
12 oz tofu, sliced
¼ cup carrots, sliced

Directions:
1. Heat the olive oil in a large saucepan over medium heat and cook the onion, kimchi, and sugar for about 5 minutes.

2. Pour the vegetable stock into the pot as well as the sweet potato.

3. Cover the pot and simmer for about 15 minutes, until the sweet potato softens.

4. Add cabbage, tofu, mushrooms, and carrots. Cook for an additional 10 minutes and serve with crusty bread.

Kimchi Fried Rice with Squid and Poached Egg

Makes 4 servings

Ingredients:
2 tablespoons canola oil
1 lb squid, cleaned and pieced
1 cup kimchi
¼ cup water
3 cups white rice, cooked
2 scallions, chopped
4 large eggs
1 tablespoon sesame oil
1 tablespoon toasted sesame seeds
½ teaspoon salt
Some ground pepper for garnishing as per taste

Directions:
1. Heat canola oil in a saucepan over medium heat.
2. Slide in the squid pieces and spread out in the pan.
3. Sprinkle with salt and cook for about 60 seconds until browned. Once done, set the squid aside in a bowl.
4. Heat sesame oil in the same pan over medium heat. Add kimchi, scallions, and water, and cook for 2–3 minutes.
5. Add rice and cook covered for about 7–8 minutes, until the liquid evaporates.
6. Add the squid back to the pan and cook for 1 minute.
7. Transfer this mixture into 4 separate bowls.
8. In the meantime, heat some water in a large saucepan until just before simmering. Do not let it reach the point of simmering—keep the heat low.

9. Gently crack each egg into the saucepan and let cook for about 1 minute. Take poached eggs out using a flat spoon and place one on top of each bowl.

10. Season with pepper and serve.

Spicy Kimchi and Chicken Noodles

Makes 4 servings

Ingredients:
1 tablespoon bouillon
2 cups kimchi
3–4 tablespoons spicy garlic sauce
1 cup shitake mushrooms, sliced
4 oz chicken leg pieces, sliced
3 cups ramen noodles
½ teaspoon salt
2 medium onions, thinly sliced
2 tablespoons salsa
2 tablespoons olive oil

Directions:
1. Boil some water in a large saucepan. Add noodles, cover with lid, and cook for 5–6 minutes. Once cooked, drain water and set aside.

2. Heat olive oil in a saucepan over medium heat.

3. Add garlic sauce and sliced onions and sauté for 2–3 minutes until the onions start to brown.

4. Throw in the shitake mushrooms and chicken pieces and cook for 3–4 minutes. Add salsa, bouillon cube, kimchi, salt, and mix well.

5. Gently slide the noodles into the saucepan and toss well with the chicken mixture. Cook for 2–3 minutes.

6. Serve hot.

Stir-Fry with Brown Rice

Makes 4 servings

Ingredients:
2 cups brown rice, cooked
1 lb lean skirt steak, cut into strips
1 cup red bell pepper, cut into strips
1 cup onions, cut into strips
1 cup carrots, shredded
1 cup Romano beans
1 tablespoon soy sauce
½ cup kimchi
1 tablespoon peanut oil
1 cup broccoli florets, chopped

Directions:

1. Heat the oil in a skillet over medium-high heat and add the steak, cooking for about 10 minutes.

2. Remove the meat and add the pepper, onions, carrots, beans, and broccoli to the skillet.

3. Add the soy sauce and toss everything together, stirring until cooked.

4. Return the steak to the skillet and add the kimchi. Stir all the ingredients together until heated and combined.

5. Place over a pile of brown rice, which should have been cooked according to package directions.

Salsa

Baked Salsa Chicken

This is one of the easiest meals you can make. Just put everything into a slow cooker, and voila! Dinner. While fermented salsa is added to the meal, the cooking process will actually kill off the beneficial probiotics. So consider topping the final product with some fermented salsa to regain those probiotics.

Makes 4 servings

Ingredients:
3 cups corn (fresh or frozen kernels)
15 oz canned black beans, drained and rinsed
15 oz canned tomatoes, diced and drained
1 cup salsa
2 garlic cloves, minced
½ teaspoon cumin
2 lbs chicken breasts, boneless and skinless
Salt and pepper to taste
Corn tortillas
Cilantro and avocados for serving

Directions:
1. In a slow cooker, add chicken breasts. Then cover with the corn, black beans, tomatoes, salsa, garlic, and cumin. Season with salt and pepper to taste.
2. Turn on the slow cooker and cook on low for 4 hours.
3. Remove the chicken and shred it with two forks.
4. Add the chicken back to the slow cooker and cook for an additional 15 minutes.
5. Serve on tortillas and top with cilantro and avocados.

Roasted Sweet Potatoes with Poached Eggs

Makes 2 servings

Ingredients:
2 sweet potatoes, scrubbed
2 teaspoons extra virgin olive oil
1 garlic clove, minced
1 tablespoon white onion, minced
⅓ cup bell pepper, diced
⅓ cup cherry tomatoes, diced
1 tablespoon parsley, minced
⅛ teaspoon black pepper
⅛ teaspoon paprika
Salt to taste
2 eggs
Salsa to serve

Directions:
1. Preheat your oven to 400°F.
2. Line a large baking sheet with parchment paper. Prepare the potatoes by pricking them all over with a fork. Place them on the baking sheet and bake for 45–60 minutes until soft. Then cut in half like a jacket potato.
3. In a sauté pan, add garlic, onion, peppers, tomatoes, and parsley with 1 teaspoon of olive oil. Cook on medium heat for a minute before seasoning with salt, pepper, and paprika. Sauté until onions are softened and the vegetables are fragrant. Set aside.
4. In a small pot, add a couple of cups of water and bring to a boil. Add a tablespoon of white vinegar, then reduce the heat to a gentle simmer. Crack one egg and place it in a small bowl. Stir the pot, creating a small whirlpool, and then slip the egg into the whirlpool. Poach the egg for 4 minutes, then remove with a slotted spoon. Blot dry, then repeat with the second egg.

5. Place each sweet potato on a plate. Top with the veggies and the poached egg. Top with fermented salsa and parsley. Serve and enjoy!

Cod with Lime and Salsa

Makes 4 servings
Ingredients:
2 lbs fresh cod
1 tablespoon olive oil
2 limes
1 cup fermented salsa
Salt and pepper to taste

Directions:
1. Preheat oven to 375°F.
2. Slice limes and layer on the bottom of a baking dish.
3. Place the cod on top of the lime slices. Drizzle with olive oil, salt, and pepper. Cook in the oven for 20 minutes or until the fish turns flaky.
4. Remove from the oven and allow to cool for five minutes.
5. Spoon salsa on top of fish.
6. This recipe pairs nicely with a salad or any crisp vegetable.

Salsa Meatloaf

Makes 10 servings

Ingredients:

2 lbs ground turkey
1 cup fermented salsa
1 cup bread crumbs
1 large onion, chopped
3 garlic cloves, minced
1 large egg
½ teaspoon salt
1½ cups chicken broth
½ teaspoon ground pepper

Directions:

1. In a bowl, combine salsa with chicken broth and bread crumbs, and mix well using a spoon. Set aside.
2. In another bowl, combine onions with minced garlic, ground turkey, and egg, and give it a mix. Now, transfer the salsa mixture to this bowl and mix again.
3. Preheat the oven to 350°F.
4. Take a loaf-shaped pan and grease it with some butter. Pour the mixture into the pan and cover with foil. Bake for about 60 minutes, until all the ingredients are cooked. Let stand for a few moments to cool down.
5. Slice and serve.

Breakfast Burrito

Makes 4 servings

Ingredients:
6 eggs
1 cup fermented salsa
1 tablespoon olive oil
1 tablespoon water
¼ cup red onion, diced
1 clove garlic, minced
½ cup bell pepper, diced
½ cup shredded cheddar cheese
½ cup sour cream
4 whole-wheat tortillas
Salt and pepper

Directions:
1. Whisk the eggs with water, salt, and pepper.
2. In a skillet, cook the garlic, onion, and bell pepper in olive oil.
3. Scramble the eggs in the skillet with the vegetables.
4. Cover the tortillas with shredded cheese.
5. Pour the egg mixture evenly into each tortilla. Top with sour cream and salsa.

Tropical Chicken Bowl

Makes 2 servings
Ingredients:
1 cup brown rice
2 cups chopped chicken, cooked
½ cup red onion, chopped
1 cup black beans, cooked
1 cup yellow corn, cooked
1 cup fermented salsa
¼ cup sour cream

Directions:
1. Cook the brown rice according to your directions, and drain.
2. In a bowl, create layers of rice, beans, chicken, onion, corn, salsa, and sour cream.

Bean Soup with Salsa

Makes 4 servings

Ingredients:
16 oz black beans, soaked overnight
1 cup chicken broth
1 tablespoon olive oil
1 onion, chopped
1 teaspoon minced garlic cloves
16 oz fermented salsa
2 tablespoons lime juice
2 teaspoons cumin powder
½ teaspoon salt
½ teaspoon paprika
2 tablespoons yogurt
Some freshly plucked cilantro leaves

Directions:
1. Boil some water in a saucepan. Add black beans and cover with a lid. Boil for about 15 minutes until the beans are thoroughly cooked. Remove from heat. Drain water and transfer beans to a food processor. Give it a whirl until it forms a paste. Set aside.
2. Heat the olive oil in a saucepan over medium-high heat.
3. Add minced garlic and onion and sauté for 2–3 minutes until the onion turns slightly brown.
4. Pour in the bean mixture, add salt, and cook for 3–4 minutes.
5. Add salsa, lime juice, chicken broth, cumin powder, and paprika and stir well using a large spoon. Bring the mixture to a boil.
6. Reduce heat and cook for another 20–25 minutes over low heat.
7. Garnish with chopped cilantro leaves, top it off with some yogurt and serve.

Conclusion

Now that you've learned all about the fermentation process, how do you feel about it? Confident that you can ferment vegetables at home? I hope so. I love making my own fermented vegetables. I find them simple and easy to care for, and they offer an excellent way of getting vegetables in the wintertime when I don't want to pay an arm and a leg for fresh vegetables.

For me, fermentation is all about the taste, but I can't deny that the health benefits are also quite amazing. Adding fermented vegetables to your diet can improve your gut health, which in turn can support other systems in your body like your immune system and mental health.

This book has taught you all the key steps you need to ferment vegetables at home. You know how important the environment is for the fermentation process, and you now know how to make the perfect fermentation environment. You've learned what equipment you'll need and also what to look out for when making your fermented vegetables. You also know how to store them.

You learned how to make several different fermented vegetables, including sauerkraut, pickles, kimchi, and salsa. To remind you, you can interchange the ingredients in these recipes. With fermentation, you're not limited with the vegetables you use, so explore different options. Finally, you learned some ideas for using fermented vegetables in meals. I hope you try out those recipes and that your fermented vegetables add a wonderful kick to the meals. Also, imagine the bragging rights when you say you made the entire meal from scratch!

Good luck with all of your fermenting at home, and remember to enjoy all that good bacteria.

Finally, I want to thank you for reading my book. If you enjoyed the book, please share your thoughts and post a review on the book retailer's website. It would be greatly appreciated!

Best wishes,
Melanie Bennet